First published 1998 © Robert Frederick Ltd.,
4 North Parade, Bath BA1 1LF

Printed and bound in China

TO A VERY SPECIAL

DAUGHTER

Saint Cecilia by John William Waterhouse (1849-1917)
Private Collection/Fine Art Photographs

"Nothing is so strong as gentleness, and nothing is so gentle as real strength."

Ralph W. Sockman

"A beautiful face is of all spectacles the most beautiful."

Jean de la Bruyère

"To believe is to be strong. Doubt cramps energy. Belief is power."

Frederick William Robertson

"A friend is a person with whom I may be sincere.
Before him I may think aloud."

Ralph Waldo Emerson

"Marriage is popular because it combines the maximum of temptation
with the maximum of opportunity."

Shelley

"God will never separate us from his love."

Paul, 1st Century

"Love Virtue, she alone is free,
She can teach ye how to climb
Higher than the sphery chime;
Or, if Virtue feeble were,
Heav'n itself would stoop to her."

Milton

"This is the secret of joy. We shall no longer strive for our own way;
but commit ourselves, easily and simply, to God's way, acquiesce in his will
and in so doing find our peace."

Evelyn Underhill

"A kiss, when all is said, what is it?
An oath that's given closer than before;
A promise more precise; the sealing of
Confessions that till then were barely breathed;
A rosy dot placed on the *i* in loving."

Edmond Rostand: Cyrano de Bergerac

Madeline After Prayer
by Daniel Maclise

Dancers in Blue
by Edgar Degas

"God is love, and whoever lives in love lives in union with God,
and God lives in union with him."

John, 1st Century

"To wait for luck is the same as waiting for death."

Author Unidentified

"The reason we all like to think so well of others is that we are all afraid of
ourselves. The basis of optimism is sheer terror."

Oscar Wilde: The Picture Of Dorian Grey

"Grace is the absence of everything that indicates pain or
difficulty, hesitation or incongruity."

William Hazlitt

"Nothing flatters a man as much as the happiness of his wife;
he is always proud of himself as the source of it."

Samuel Johnson

"Sincerity is the highest compliment you can pay."

Ralph Waldo Emerson

"Those graces which from their presumed facility encourage all to attempt an imitation of them, are usually the most inimitable."

C. C. Colton

"He who binds to himself a joy
Does the winged life destroy;
But he who kisses the joy as it flies
Lives in eternity's sunrise."

William Blake

"Often the difference between a successful marriage and a mediocre one consists of leaving about three or four things a day unsaid."

Harlan Miller

"He who does not hope to win has already lost."

Jose Joaquin Olmedo

The Shrine by John William
Waterhouse (1849-1917)
Christopher Wood Gallery,
London/Bridgeman Art Library,
London

"You Cannot Barre Love Oute"
by Arthur Hughes (1832-1915)
Sotheby's Picture Library

"Virtue is the roughest way,
But proves at night a bed of down."
Sir Henry Wotton

"Our knowledge is a receding mirage in an expanding desert of ignorance."
Will Durant

"Perfect love leaves no room for fear."
John, 1st Century

"There's nothing worth the wear of winning,
But laughter and the love of friends."
Hilaire Belloc

"Good luck comes to the saucy and bold."
Welsh Proverb

"Marriage is like life in this – that it is a field of battle, and not a bed of roses."
Robert Louis Stevenson

"An optimist sees an opportunity in every calamity:
a pessimist sees a calamity in every opportunity."
Author Unidentified

"The proper office of a friend is to side with you when you are in the wrong.
Nearly anybody will side with you when you are in the right."
Mark Twain

"As we acquire more knowledge, things do not become
more comprehensible, but more mysterious."
Albert Schweitzer

"God could not be everywhere, so He made mothers."
Jewish Proverb

"I never knew an early-rising, hard-working, prudent man, careful of his
earnings, and strictly honest, who complained of bad luck."
Joseph Addison

Venetian Ladies Listening to the Serenade
by Frank Cadogan Cowper (1877-1958)
Sotheby's Picture Library

Roses on a Riverbank by Madeleine Lemaire (1845-1928)
Sotheby's Picture Library

"A wise man sings his joy in the closet of his heart."

Tibullus

"Men always want to be a woman's first love; women have a more
subtle instinct: what they like is to be a man's last romance."

Author Unidentified

"To look up and not down,
To look forward and not back,
To look out and not in, and
To lend a hand."

E. E. Hale

"We never know the love of our parents for us till we have become parents."

Henry Ward Beecher

"The magic of first love is our ignorance that it can ever end."

Benjamin Disraeli

"Marriage is three parts love and seven parts forgiveness of sins."

Langdon Mitchell

"Respect a man, he will do the more."

James Howell

"The first duty of a wise advocate is to convince his opponents that he understands their arguments, and sympathises with their just feelings."

Samuel Taylor Coleridge

"Your friend is the man who knows all about you and still likes you."

Elbert Hubbard

"Who never climbed high never fell low."

Thomas Fuller

"Treasure the love you receive above all. It will survive long after your gold and good health have vanished."

Og Mandino

Proserpine
by Dante Gabriel Rossetti

Women with Umberella Turned to the Right
by Claude Monet

"Modesty ought to be the virtue of those who are deficient in other virtues."

Stanislaus Leszcynski, King of Poland

"Who, being loved, is poor?"

Oscar Wilde

"I don't know anything about luck. I've never banked on it,
and I'm afraid of people who do. Luck to me is something else: hard work
and realising what is opportunity and what isn't."

Lucille Ball

"Womanliness means only motherhood;
All love begins and ends there."

Robert Browning

"The joys of parents are secret, and so are their griefs and fears:
they cannot utter the one, nor they will not utter the other."

Francis Bacon

"Virtue is bold, and goodness never fearful."
Shakespeare: Measure for Measure

"All ambitions are lawful except those which climb upward
on the miseries or credulities of mankind."
Joseph Conrad

"Marriage is not a finished affair. No matter to what age you live,
love must be continuously consolidated. Being considerate, thoughtful and
respectful without ulterior motives is the key to a successful marriage."
Pamphlet from Chinese Family Planning Centre

"A happy bridesmaid makes a happy bride."
Lord Tennyson

"You will find as you look back upon your life that the moments when you have
really lived are the moments when you have done things in the spirit of love."
Henry Drummond

Poppies at Argenteuil by Claude Monet

The Year's at Spring,
All's right with the World
by Sir Lawrence Alma-Tadema (1836-1912)
Sotheby's Picture Library

"For an instant, love can transform the world."
Author Unidentified

"Honesty is the first chapter in the book of wisdom."
Thomas Jefferson

"The fountains mingle with the river
And the rivers with the Ocean,
The winds of heaven mix for ever
With a sweet emotion;
Nothing in the world is single;
All things by a law divine
In one spirit meet and mingle,
Why not I with thine?"
Shelley

"A kiss can be a comma, a question mark or an exclamation point.
That's basic spelling that every woman ought to know."
Mistinguett

"To know that we know what we know,
and that we do not know what we do not know,
that is true knowledge."
Henry David Thoreau

"We are all born for love; it is the principle of existence and its only end."
Benjamin Disraeli

"Some folk want their luck buttered."
Thomas Hardy: The Mayor of Casterbridge

"Modesty is the only sure bait when you angle for praise."
Lord Chesterfield

"When I was a boy of fourteen, my father was so ignorant
I could hardly stand to have the old man around.
But when I got to be twenty one, I was astonished at how much
he had learned in seven years."
Mark Twain

The Musicians
in the Orchestra
by Edgar Degas

Summer by Sir William Ernest Reynold-Stephens (1862-1943)
Whitford & Hughes, London/Bridgeman Art Library, London

"A pessimist is a man who thinks all women are bad.
An optimist is the one who hopes they are."

Chauncey Depew

"Mother is the name for God in the lips and hearts of little children."

W. M. Thackeray: Vanity Fair

"Since the house is on fire, let us warm ourselves."

Italian Proverb

"Joy is for all men. It does not depend on circumstance or condition."

Horace Bushnell

"I keep my friends as misers do their treasure, because, of all the things
granted us by wisdom, none is greater or better than friendship."

Pietro Aretino

"Good luck is a lazy man's estimate of a worker's success."

Author Unidentified

"Unable are the Loved to die
For Love is Immortality."
Emily Dickinson

"Marriage is an empty box. It remains empty unless you put in
more than you take out."
Author Unidentified

"Love, all alike, no season knows, nor clime,
Nor hours, age, months, which are the rags of time."
John Donne

"The superior man is distressed by the limitations of his ability;
he is not distressed by the fact that men do not recognise the ability he has."
Confucius

"Good nature is worth more than knowledge, more than money,
more than honour, to the persons who possess it."
Henry Ward Beecher

'I am Half Sick of Shadows,' said
the Lady of Shalott (1915)
by John William Waterhouse

Springtime by Claude Monet

"To know a little of anything gives neither satisfaction nor credit,
but often brings disgrace and ridicule."

Lord Chesterfield

"The man who has never made a fool of himself in love
will never be wise in love."

Theodor Reik

"Love feeds on hope, they say, or love will die – Ah miserie!
Yet my love lives, although no hope have I! – Ah miserie!"

W. S. Gilbert

"When you tell the truth, you never have to worry about your lousy memory."

Author Unidentified

"As a wife you may be your husband's salvation;
as a husband you may be your wife's salvation."

1 Corinthians 7:16

"Nothing is good or bad, but thinking makes it so."
Shakespeare

"Never has there been one possessed of complete sincerity
who did not move others. Never has there been one who had not sincerity
who was able to move others."
Mencius

"Modesty is of no use to a beggar."
Homer

" 'Lord, how often am I to forgive my brother if he goes on wronging me?
As often as seven times?' Jesus replied, 'I do not say seven times;
I say seventy times seven'."
Matthew 18:21-22

"Train up a child in the way he should go, and when he is old,
he will not depart from it."
Proverbs 22:6
Miranda – The Tempest by John William Waterhouse (1849-1917)
Sotheby's Picture Library

The Awakening of Love by
Gustave Schmatz Herbert
Christies Photo Library,
London

"Of cheerfulness, or a good temper –
the more it is spent, the more of it remains."
Ralph Waldo Emerson

"Don't carry a grudge. While you're carrying the grudge
the other guy's out dancing."
Buddy Hackett

"No legacy is so rich as honesty."
Shakespeare: All's Well That Ends Well

"When you have been wronged, a poor memory is your best response."
Author Unidentified

"A little learning is a dangerous thing."
Alexander Pope

"Immature love says: 'I love you because I need you.'
Mature love says: 'I need you because I love you.' "
Erich Fromm

"The love we give away is the only love we keep."

Elbert Hubbard

"An ideal wife is any woman who has an ideal husband."

Booth Tarkington

"Confidence in an unfaithful man in time of trouble
is like a broken tooth, and a foot out of joint."

Proverbs 25:19

"Love is an act of endless forgiveness, a tender look which becomes a habit."

Peter Ustinov

"To be without some of the things you want is an
'indispensable part of happiness."

Bertrand Russell

"Most people are about as happy as they make up their minds to be."

Abraham Lincoln

Divinely Fair, 1893,
by Henry Thomas
Schafer (1873-1915)
Sotheby's Picture
Library

The Empress Comes (or
"Poppea Comes") by George
Lawrence (1858-1933)
Sotheby's Picture Library

"Dishonesty is like a boomerang. About the time you think all is well, it hits you in the back of the head."

Author Unidentified

"One word
Frees us of all the weight and pain of life:
That word is love."

Sophocles

"All that mankind has ever learned is nothing more than a single grain of sand on a beach that reaches to infinity."

Author Unidentified

"By all means marry; if you have a good wife, you'll become happy; if you have a bad one, you'll become a philosopher."

Socrates

"Don't let what you cannot do interfere with what you can do."

John Wooden

"To be patient shows great understanding;
quick temper is the height of folly."

Proverbs 14:29

"If you have some respect for people as they are, you can be more effective
in helping them to become better than they are."

John W. Gardner

"They can conquer who believe they can."

John Dryden

"We pardon as long as we love."

François de la Rochefoucauld

"There is no more lovely, friendly and charming relationship,
communion or company than a good marriage."

Martin Luther

Le Moulin de la Galette
by Augusté Renoir.

"Love and war are the same thing, and stratagems and policy
are as allowable in the one as the other."
Cervantes: Don Quixote

"Happiness seems to require a modicum of external prosperity."
Aristotle

"All love is sweet,
Given or returned. Common as light is love,
And its familiar voice wearies not ever."
Shelley

"To feed men and not to love them is to treat them as if they were
barnyard cattle. To love them and not to respect them is to treat
them as if they were household pets."
Mencius

"Absence sharpens love; presence strengthens it."
Thomas Fuller

"Some men are just as firmly convinced of what they
think as others are of what they know."
Aristotle

"The ineffable joy of forgiving and being forgiven forms an ecstasy
that might well arouse the envy of the gods."
Elbert Hubbard

"They also serve who only stand and wait."
John Milton

"Modesty gives the maid greater beauty than even the bloom of youth,
it bestows on the wife the dignity of a matron, and reinstates
the widow in her virginity."
Joseph Addison

"No man who has once heartily and wholly laughed
can be altogether irreclaimably bad."
Thomas Carlyle

Ophelia,
by John William
Waterhouse

Youth by Sir Lawrence Alma-Tadema (1836-1912)
Sotheby's Picture Library

"There is only one good, knowledge, and one evil, ignorance."
Socrates

"The chains of marriage are so heavy that it takes two to bear them,
sometimes three."
Alexandre Dumas fils

"Have patience with all things, but chiefly have patience with yourself.
Do not lose courage in considering your own imperfections, but instantly set
about remedying them – every day begin the task anew."
Ascribed to St. Francis de Sales

"The goal of education is the advancement of knowledge
and the dissemination of truth."
John F. Kennedy

"Sometimes when one person is missing, the whole world seems depopulated."
Lamartine

"Correction does much, but encouragement does more."
Johann Wolfgang von Goethe

"'Tis better to have loved and lost,
Than never to have loved at all."
Alfred Tennyson

"Laughter has no foreign accent."
Paul Lowney

"Love is a conflict between reflexes and reflections."
Magnus Hirschfield

"Well-married, a man is winged – ill-matched, he is shackled."
Henry Ward Beecher

"In love, pain and pleasure are always at war."
Publilius Syrus

Beads, 1880 by Albert Moore (1841-93)
National Gallery of Scotland, Edinburgh/Bridgeman Art Library, London

Summer Scape by Auguste Renoir

"Our hours in love have wings; in absence crutches."
Colley Cibber

"Courtesy wins woman all as well
As valour may, but he that closes both
Is perfect."
Lord Tennyson

"The world's greatest men have not commonly been great scholars,
nor its great scholars great men."
Oliver Wendell Holmes

"A merry heart goes all the day
Your sad tires in a mile-a."
Shakespeare: The Winter's Tale

"Love doesn't sit there like a stone, it has to be made, like bread;
remade all the time, made new."
Ursula K. le Guin

"A man's wife has more power over him than the state has."
Ralph Waldo Emerson

"Grief can take care of itself, but to get the full value of joy you must have somebody to divide it with."
Mark Twain

"He is not laughed at that laughs at himself first."
Thomas Fuller

"Each of our leading conceptions – each branch of our knowledge – passes successively through three different theoretical conditions: the theological, or fictitius; the metaphysical, or abstract; the scientific, or positive."
Auguste Comte

"She will never win him, whose
Words had shown she feared to lose."
Dorothy Parker

Two Dancers on the Stage
by Edgar Degas

The Quay at Bougival
by Berthe Morisot

"If love lives on hope, it dies with it; it is a fire which goes out for want of fuel."

Pierre Cornielle: The Cid

"Any married man should forget his mistakes –
no use two people remembering the same thing."

Duane Dewel

"We have no more right to consume happiness without producing it
than to consume wealth without producing it."

George Bernard Shaw

"Only two things are necessary to keep one's wife happy.
One is to let her think she is having her own way, and the other,
to let her have it."

Lyndon B. Johnson

"One can know a man from his laugh, and if you like a man's laugh before you
know anything of him, you may confidently say that he is a good man."

Dostoevsky

"Those undeserved joys which come uncalled and make us more pleased
than grateful are they that sing."

Thoreau

"Happiness makes up in height for what it lacks in length."

Robert Frost

"Life doesn't come with an instruction book – that's why we have fathers."

Author Unidentified

"Adapt or perish, now as ever, is Nature's inexorable imperative."

H. G. Wells

"Wondrous is the strength of cheerfulness, and its power of endurance –
the cheerful man will do more in the same time, will do it better, will persevere
in it longer than the sad or sullen."

Thomas Carlyle

"The most wasted day is that in which we have not laughed."

Chamfort

The Artist's Garden, Irises
by Claude Monet